# SIMPLY DRAWING

*Jacqui Grantford*

Published by Hinkler Books Pty Ltd
45–55 Fairchild Street
Heatherton Victoria 3202 Australia
www.hinkler.com.au

hinkler

Author: Jacqui Grantford
Project Editor: Katie Hewat
Cover Design: Hinkler Design Studio
Internal Design: Pandemonium Creative
Photography: Ned Meldrum
Prepress: Graphic Print Group

ISBN: 978 1 7418 4776 5

Printed and bound in China

# Contents

# Introduction

Welcome to *Simply Drawing*.

There's something thoroughly satisfying about creating a great drawing. It's something that lasts forever and is an expression of who you are. Learning to draw teaches you about the world around you and develops dexterity of mind and hand.

Sometimes it can seem daunting and the catchphrase 'I can't draw' is commonly heard from people who don't draw regularly. We're going to simplify the whole process of drawing and make it an achievable and absorbing exercise.

Throughout this book we'll explore everything you need to begin in the amazing world of drawing.

# Materials Needed

One of the great things about the materials needed for drawing is that very little is required.

The following materials are the basics from which you can then expand and explore once you feel you have mastered the beginnings of drawing.

## Pencils

Pencils come in a variety of tones. The following is a scale from dark and soft to light and hard. 'H' stands for hard, 'B' for black and 'F' for fine point.

| Dark < 6B  5B  4B  3B  2B  B  HB  F  H  2H  3H  4H  5H  6H > **Light** |
|---|

To start, you wouldn't need all these variations. I would use 2H, HB, 2B, 3B, 4B and 6B.

Later on you'll expand the types of drawing materials to include the full range when necessary and other types of medium like graphite, charcoal, conte, pastels and many more. There's a whole heap of fun ahead experimenting with art materials once you've mastered the basics.

## Erasers

Vinyl erasers are great for removing most of the marks on your paper. Kneadable erasers are great for lifting out highlights and pulling back some of the dark bits if you need to. You can mould them into any shape, giving you a fair degree of accuracy for tricky, fine bits.

# Easels

There are many types of easels. You can visit your art shop to view all the different varieties. I would only stress that you make sure your easel is stable. There's nothing more frustrating than drawing on a wobbly surface.

Some people prefer to draw standing up so they can move as they draw and readily stand back from their work to view it. That's my personal preference. Others prefer to sit, in which case a drafting table would be better.

If you don't have an easel or a drafting table, don't let it stop you from drawing. You can easily draw sitting at the kitchen table, or under a tree on a lovely spring day. There is no right or wrong – merely what works for you.

# Boards

You will need a board that is bigger than the paper you are working on. Sometimes leaving extra space to pin up roughs or references can be handy.

The paper can be attached with either masking tape or a bulldog clip. The advantage of masking tape is that you can move the paper around if you want.

# Stanley knife

Using a Stanley knife is a really effective way to sharpen your pencil. You have greater control than with a normal sharpener because you can vary the amount of lead that shows for different width strokes. Scalpels can also be used, but I feel that Stanley knives are a little safer, especially if you have small children in the household, as you can wind these knives back down.

# Sandpaper pad

You can use a single sheet of sandpaper attached to your board, or a sandpaper pad to sharpen or blunt the end of your pencil depending on the particular result you're after.

# Paper stumps

These are pieces of paper rolled up into a solid stump and then sharpened at both ends. They're great for blending your work, or softening the pencil line.

# Paper

Cartridge paper is a great paper to start with. It's inexpensive, comes in various sizes and has a good medium, smooth surface. Once you're comfortable with the basic skills you'll have lots of fun experimenting with other papers with different textures and colours.

# Scrap paper

It's handy to have a piece of scrap paper attached to your board to clean your eraser before you use it, otherwise it can leave marks on your paper. The paper can also be used to fine-tune the point of your pencil and test if it's the right bluntness or sharpness for the marks you're about to make.

Another spare piece of paper is handy to lean on, so you don't smudge your work.

# Sketchbook or visual diary

These are terrific for location drawing. Most of your development will come from drawing what you see. You can take the book with you anywhere – trips to the beach, holidays, sitting at a café drinking coffee. Lots of preliminary work can be done in your visual diary, and it's a great way to develop your visual skills.

# Framing device

You can buy ready-made framing devices or make them yourself. They are two pieces of cardboard in 'L' shapes. You can join them to make an adjustable rectangle to look through and assess the best composition.

# Hand Positions

The two main positions are:

## Handwriting position

This can be used for precision lines and careful application of tone and accents.

## Underhand position

In this hold, the pencil passes under the hand instead of over the thumb. It's great for looser lines and strokes and helps to free up your work. This is a great position for quickly sketching in large works.

## Other hand positions

There are many other ways to hold your pencil. The 'cupped hand' position is similar to the underhand position, but the whole hand turns around so that the palm faces up. The 'pencil on the side' position is the opposite and has the top of the hand facing up and the pencil held loosely in the fingers, not touching the hand at all. There's also the 'fencing foil' position, which has the fingers curled around the pencil like a sword.

Have fun changing positions, but focus on the main two in the beginning. The important thing is to make sure you're relaxed when you hold the pencil and that it feels comfortable and natural.

**Cupped hand position**

**Pencil on the side position**

**Fencing foil position**

# Experiments with the Pencil

## Variations with line and texture and tone

Practise drawing straight lines freehand and then circular strokes followed by scribbles and flicked lines. See if you can create thick lines and thin lines with all the different types of leads. Also experiment with the different lines produced when your pencil is sharp and blunt. Try using the different leads laid flat to create a smooth result. Try it now on the tip of the pencil.

The following examples show a number of different ways to create texture. Even the most experienced artists are always experimenting with different ways to use the pencil.

**HB**

**2H**

**3B**

**6B**

**freehand lines**

circles

directional scribbles 2H

dots and flicks

scribbles

directional scribbles 4B

flicks

# Hatching and crosshatching

These are really useful for creating tone. Hatching is simply closely packed straight lines in a diagonal direction.

Crosshatching is when lines are laid over the top in the opposite direction and then vertically and horizontally as well. This can create a really smooth effect.

Using crosshatching, try to create a scale of tone using an HB pencil like the following example. You can follow this up with a scale that has no separations.

**HB on point**  **4B on point**  **HB flat**  **4B flat**

**hatching**  **crosshatching**

# Three Dimensions

Four basic shapes – the square, rectangle, triangle and circle – can be turned into three-dimensional objects with the illusion of line.

Starting with the square, you can add short lines of equal length to three of the corners. Make sure they are parallel and at about 45 degrees. Join those lines and you have a cube.

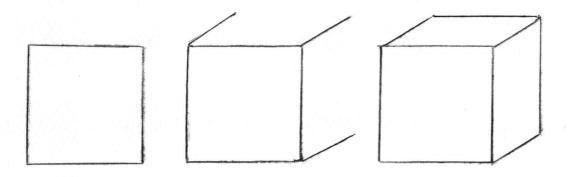

Another version of the cube is from a diamond with a longer horizontal line than vertical. Add three even parallel lines dropping down and then join them. You now have another cube, but this time the edge where the sides meet is pointing towards you.

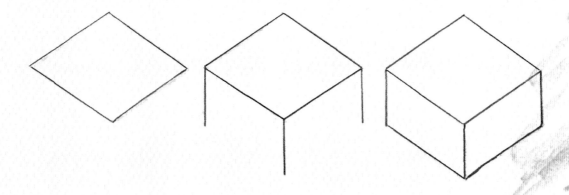

Add an ellipse to the bottom and the top of a rectangle and you have a cylinder. An ellipse is an oval shape and each quarter is the same shape and size. The best way to draw it accurately is simply through practise and using your eye to see if it looks right.

Add an ellipse to the bottom of a triangle and you have a cone.

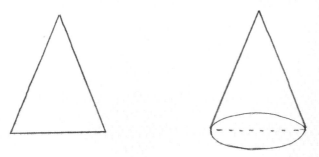

I've left the circle to last as it's a little different to the others. To turn a circle into a sphere you don't need to add any lines, but simply shading.

Start by drawing a circle and lightly shade it, leaving a white spot in the upper left corner. Make sure the shading is gradual and that the light spot is noticeably lighter. To add to the effect, fade a soft shadow away from the light side under the circle.

Now have a go at shading the other shapes as well.

# Seeing the Basic Shapes in Objects

Basic shapes can be seen in all objects around us. Sometimes they are simple and easy to recognise like the cube in a cardboard box, and sometimes they are more complex and are made up of many shapes, taking a practised eye to see.

We're going to start with simple objects where one basic shape is easy to see, such as a chess piece that is the shape of a cone.

1. Start by drawing a cone with an HB pencil. Sketch it in lightly so you can make changes without leaving any permanent marks.

2. Next, start adding the shape of the chess piece around the cone.

3. Finish off by adding small amounts of tone using the 3B and smooth it out with a 2H over the top, or use a paper stump for a more polished effect.

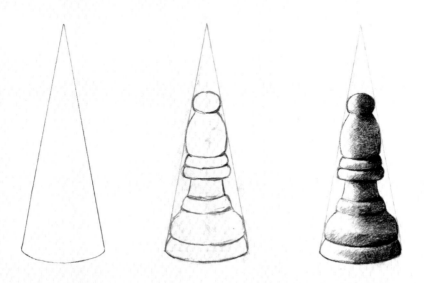

Have a look around the house and see what else you can find that fits a basic shape. It could be a clock, a camera, a long glass, a log of wood or a basketball. Have a go at drawing these following the same steps.

# Perspective

Perspective is a fabulous tool to aid our 3D effect. Have you ever noticed how a road looks smaller as it goes into the distance and seems to vanish? That is an example of perspective.

## One-point perspective

The horizon line is either the actual horizon, or whatever horizontal line is level with your eye. When two parallel lines recede into the distance, they converge towards a point. This is called the vanishing point. The following drawing demonstrates this. All the lines meet at one point.

It's also the same type of perspective we see with the road in the distance.

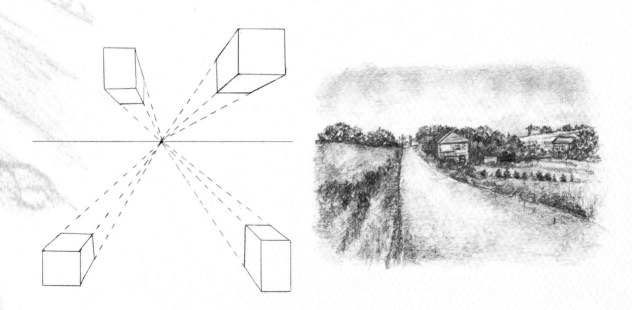

## Two-point perspective

When an object isn't at a full frontal view you will see two sides or planes. This will then have two vanishing points, one to the left and one to the right. This can also apply to everyday life.

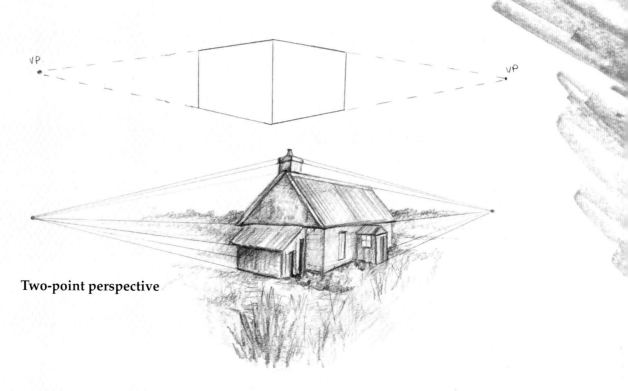

**Two-point perspective**

# Three-point perspective

If the object is viewed from an extreme angle, the vertical lines have their own vanishing point as well. This is used when you're viewing something from a very low or high point.

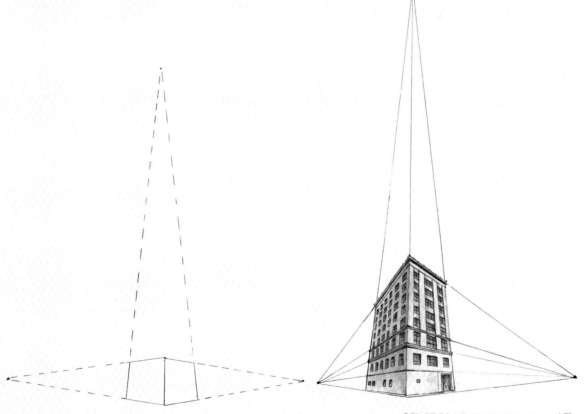

# Foreshortening

Foreshortening goes hand in hand with perspective in that things closer to you look bigger than they do in the distance. This means that we sometimes draw something that is tiny much bigger than larger things further away. Our brain makes the connection, however, and knows that the tiny thing is still little, despite being drawn larger. It just looks larger because it's closer.

This ring has been drawn in varying degrees of foreshortening, depending on your viewpoint. As we move over it, it becomes rounder. As we view it straight on, it loses its circular properties and becomes more elliptical.

The same principle applies to these drawings of hands. As the hand is pointing towards us, the fingers get shorter until they're almost like stumps.

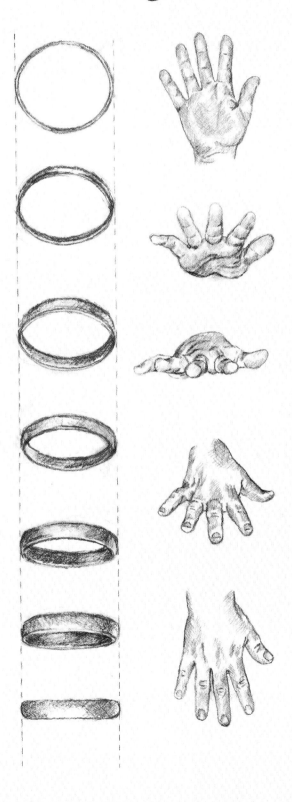

# Measuring

## Measuring grid

You can buy ready-made framing devices or make them up out of an old picture frame. Simply draw a grid on the glass of a frame that's the same proportion as your paper. This can then be used as an aid for measuring your drawing.

Lightly divide your page into the same number of squares, but make sure they're light enough to be erased later. Then, when you're drawing your picture, match up what you draw with what you see in the corresponding squares.

A good way to practise this principle is to draw a grid over a photocopy of a picture. Draw up a matching grid on a plain piece of paper and try to copy it. Using the measuring grid, follow exactly the same process.

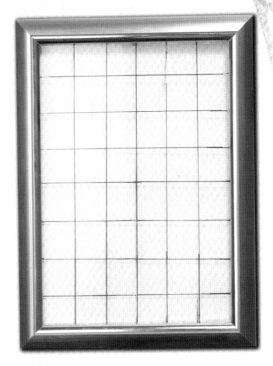

## Sight-size drawing

Hold your pencil (or ruler or anything straight) out in front of you with your arm fully extended. Close one eye and measure the first bit of the subject you wish to draw. Hold the pencil against your paper and, using a different pencil, mark that measurement on your paper. Continue this process until you have most of the main points of the drawing measured on the paper. If you want the drawing to be either bigger or smaller, simply move closer or further away from the subject.

# Cross-reference measuring

As you do more and more drawing, your eye will automatically check where the objects are in relation to each other.

Looking at the hat and the bottle, for example, you would always check where the top of the hat is in relation to the bottle. Compare the width of the bottle to the hat. Double-check how each bit measures compared to the objects around it.

Most importantly: draw what you see, not what you think you see! The measurements may not be what you expect at first, but trust them. They will make more sense once everything is together.

**Hat is about half the height of the bottle**

**Hat is about twice the width of the bottle**

# Lighting

Lighting is one of the most important tools you'll have as far as creating mood with your drawing is concerned.

If you look at the drawing of this cylinder, you'll see the different effects of lighting from the side, and from the back and the front. Also note the effect that the direction of the different lighting has on the shadows. The shadow tends to fall in the opposite direction to the source of the light.

There are two main types of lighting: natural and artificial.

## Natural light

The effect of natural light will depend largely on the time of day and the weather, so when you choose to draw will be important.

During the morning or late afternoon, the sun is lower and creates a gentle sidelight and longer shadows, bringing out the texture in objects. It's also a slightly more orange light.

**Morning light**

When the sun is at its highest, everything is lit directly overhead and it creates a harsher light on very sunny days. If you are drawing people, you can get quite strong shadows under the eyes and nose.

On slightly overcast days, the light will be softer and the look will be quite natural and flattering, but without as much contrast.

**Overhead light**        **Overcast light**

# Artificial light

When using studio light, you have much more control. Use a light or lamp so that you can manipulate the direction of the light source. And remember, the stronger the wattage, the more dramatic the effect.

Compare the differences between the two faces that are lit from the side and lit from underneath. The latter has a dark and eerie effect.

Experimenting with different lighting is great fun. It's amazing what diverse results you can get drawing the same object, but in different lighting. Choose a simple object from home – a stuffed toy, a hard-surfaced toy, a log from the garden, a candlestick or an ornament – and try drawing it in as many different lighting situations as possible.

**Lit from the side**

**Lit from below**

# Texture

Different materials have different textures and there are ways that you can show these distinct characteristics.

## Glass

Glass has white highlights reflecting the light and objects around the room. There are darker and lighter lines following the vertical direction of the glass. It's a smooth surface, so this is a case where crosshatching and smooth shading are good. You may also want to use your eraser to emphasise the highlights if necessary.

## Metal

This is another smooth surface, so will also use smooth shading. Metal has strong highlights and contrasts. Start with an HB, then add darker tones with a 3B pencil.

# Fur

You can imitate the fur using short flicks with your pencil. Patches of dark and light in sections will add to the realism.

# Rock

Use your pencil in a slightly scribbly way to imitate the rough texture of rocks. There are strong contrasts between the different planes, although the actual flat surfaces are fairly uniform in shade. Using a darker lead, add in dots and bumps to create more texture.

# Silk

The folds in silk are round and the shiny surface creates a highlight at the top of each curve. These will require smooth shading.

Creating a convincing texture requires you to look for the shadows and highlights. Many things are shiny, but where the highlights fall is what distinguishes them. Also try to imitate the smooth or rough surface with your pencil. Have fun exploring different objects and analysing their surfaces.

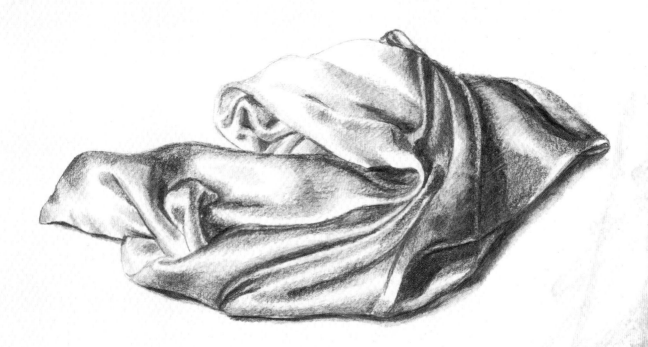

# Still Life

You have essentially been drawing still lifes with the single objects you've already drawn. But most still life compositions consist of more than one inanimate object arranged in a way that is pleasing or meaningful to the eye. You can choose things that interest you because they look quirky or fun to draw, or you might choose things that when placed together take on a symbolic meaning.

Find objects around the house that you think will work well, or visit an opportunity shop or garage sale and see if they have any old things that would suit.

Objects with a variety of different textures are often effective and provide variety within your drawing. When setting up your still life, overlapping the objects is a good way to provide depth.

This isn't always the case, however. You might wish to create a minimalist, futuristic feel and in that case you might choose objects that all look polished and arrange them sparsely.

Experiment with the positioning of the objects until you're happy with the composition.

Try different lighting on your set-up. As you have already discovered, various types of lighting will alter the whole mood of your drawing. Play around with the light till you have the effect you're after. It may be natural light through a window, or more extreme light from an artificial source.

Once you're fairly happy with your composition you can use the framing device to help you decide how to frame your work. You may decide to have the drawing going off the page, or it may all be contained within the page. Unless you are specifically trying to achieve a minimalist effect, don't do a tiny drawing in the middle of your page with lots of space around it. Use your paper to its capacity.

Draw up some quick thumbnails to check how it's all working. This is the time to work out the faults in the composition or framing. Thumbnails should be really quick. Don't spend more than five minutes on each. They're problem solvers, not finished drawings.

Now it's time to start drawing! Lightly sketch in your composition using an HB pencil. Use your measurement skills to make sure the proportions are right and everything aligns at the right spot. You can use a grid, the sight-size method of measuring, or simply use your eye to cross-reference everything. Sometimes it's good to use a sketchy style at this stage to help 'find the lines'. When a line is sketchy with lots of loose lines around it to choose from, your eye can automatically pick the right one.

Start lightly, adding tone and looking for the dark sections and the highlights. Use your pencil in ways to create the effects of the texture you are drawing.

Look for the shadows and see where they lie. Look also for the cast shadows. These are shadows on objects created by other objects. They give a sense of depth while adding to the illusion that the objects are overlapping.

Further develop the tone in your drawing with darker pencils in the dark parts and the shadows. Use the lighter pencils to smooth the transition to the lighter bits. You may even want to use the paper stump to help even out the shading. Make sure you have plenty of contrast between the lights and darks. Sometimes it's good to exaggerate this to add to the drama of your work.

Constantly stand back from your work to see how it's looking. If you want to pull the highlights out more, use the kneadable eraser.

Continue adding or pulling back tone and texture until you're satisfied with the end result.

# The Human Form

The human form can be one of the most interesting subjects to draw. When drawing figures, it's useful to have some idea of the structure of the body. In Leonardo's day, they used to dissect the body to analyse how it works. We don't need to do that, but it does help to have some idea of proportions.

It's generally accepted that the length of the head will fit seven-and-a-half times into the body. The classical proportions were eight heads to the length of the body, but many of the figures drawn in that time were god-like figures. Although this is still used today for fashion drawings and magazines, the more realistic proportions are seven-and-a-half heads to the length of the body.

The midpoint of the body is at the pubic bone, not at the waist as many people think.

The female form is more rounded with narrower shoulders and wider hips than the male.

Children have slightly different proportions to adults. Toddlers are approximately four heads tall and six- to seven-year-old children are six heads tall. By the age of ten, they are about seven heads tall.

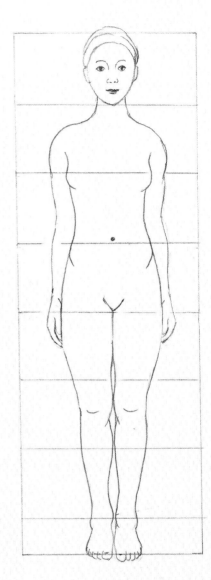

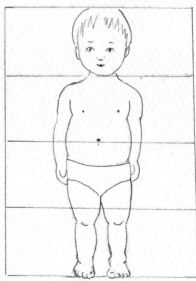

When the head is viewed straight on:

- The width of the head is about two-thirds of the height
- The eyes are halfway between the top of the head and the chin
- The bottom of the nose is halfway between the eyes and the chin
- The bottom of the mouth is halfway between the nose and the chin
- The corners of the mouth align with the centre of the eyes
- The top of the ears align with the eyebrows
- The bottom of the ears align with the bottom of the nose
- The nose is the same width as the eyes
- The eyes are one eye-width apart

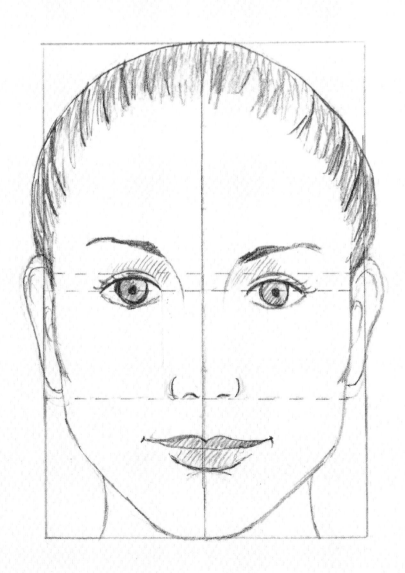

With the face in profile, the head divides in half at the jawline in front of the ears. The back of the head is deceptively larger than many people think. The only part that projects beyond this grid is the nose, which can be variable in size.

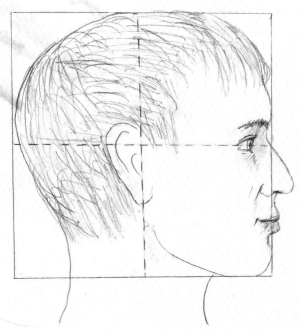

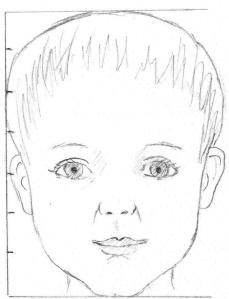

Children and babies have a proportionally larger forehead. With a baby, you'll find the middle of the eyes is three-sevenths up the face. The lower lip is on the first seventh and the nose is on the next.

These are, of course, generalisations and with all these proportions and characteristics it's important to double-check what you're drawing from your model and reference and see if it really is what you're seeing, especially once you start drawing heads from all sorts of angles. That's when foreshortening distorts proportions and your eye is the best tool you have.

**Three-quarter profile**

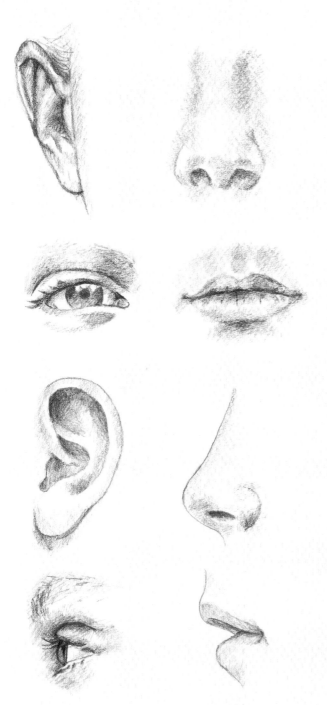

# Characteristics and expressions

### The face front on
The lips have two peaks and a dent on the upper lip under the nose. The line where the lips meet should mostly be a darker line than the outside of the lips. Only part of the ears can be seen. And although it may seem silly, don't forget to draw the eyelids if they're visible. Many beginners forget that we have eyelids and compensate with really big eyelashes.

### The face in profile
The eyes in profile are a completely different shape to when they are viewed front on and look roughly similar to a triangle. The mouth is half the length, so make sure you don't draw it too long. The eyes do not go above the nose in profile. This is a common mistake.

### The face in three-quarter view
When drawing the face at three-quarter view, the eye furthest away will be a different shape and will appear much shorter. The half of the mouth furthest away will also be smaller, as will part of the nose.

Drawing different expressions can be one of the most enjoyable drawing experiences. Everyone can connect with human emotions, so immediately you're creating something your viewing audience will relate to.

### Shocked
The eyes are wide and staring, with the whole iris visible. Wrinkles will often appear in the forehead from raised eyebrows and the mouth will be loosely open.

### Happy
The mouth turns up, showing teeth, which raises the cheeks and in turn crinkles the eyes. Eyebrows tend to stay neutral.

### Angry
The eyes will be narrowed, with the brows drawn together causing frown lines. The mouth turns down and lines will travel down from the corners of the mouth.

There's a whole multitude of different expressions. Search different expressions on the internet and see what common characteristics you can find, or ask your friends and family to pull faces for you.

**Shocked**

**Happy**

**Angry**

## Hands and feet

A lot of people avoid hands and feet, thinking that they're harder than everything else. They're not. You just need to break them down into simple elements and practise drawing them.

The middle finger on our hands is only slightly shorter than the length of the palm. Our whole hand is as long as the length from our chin to near the top of our forehead. People often make the mistake of drawing hands too small.

The best way to get used to drawing hands is to practise in as many different positions as possible. Always mark in the knuckles as they give the bends and contours.

The feet are approximately the size of our head. The ankle bone is larger on the outside of the foot than the inside and these bones are important in making the foot look real. The large toe goes into the rest of the foot about four times and, of course, the other toes get smaller.

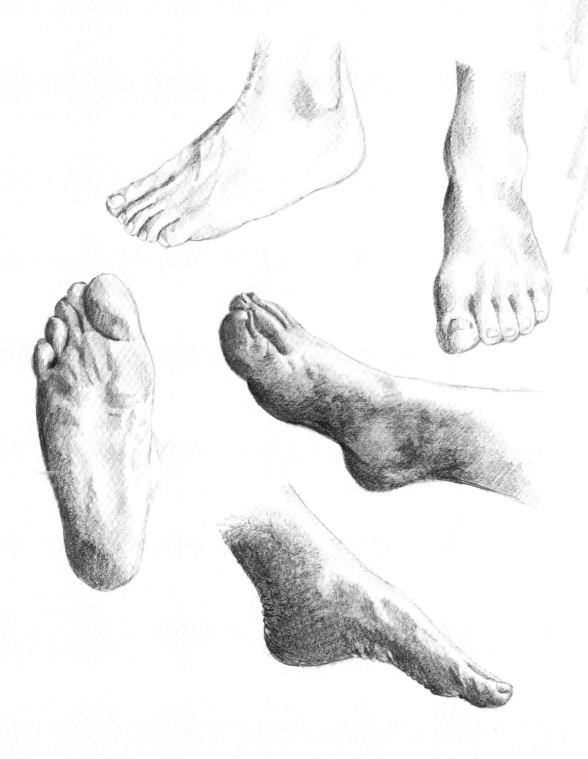

# Drawing the figure

Ask people to model for you, or see if you can get to a life class. Drawing the naked form is one of the best ways to tune your eye … although your friends will probably want to keep their clothes on. Otherwise, use photos as references to start with.

In this illustration the figure is standing. Like the still life I drew before, I started lightly sketching in the proportions of my model using my measuring skills. Knowing the basic rules of proportions was also helpful to double-check that my measurements made sense.

I then lightly shaded in the figure and, once I was happy that my main areas of shading were correct, continued with different leads to emphasise the darks and the lights.

The same formula applies here. Check that your figure is balanced. Male figures can have lots of muscle tone, so look for all the subtle variations that you can shade. Sometimes your knowledge of proportions will have to be modified due to foreshortening. This is where your eye and ability to measure will be important.

# Foreshortening the human form

Often when drawing the human form, the rules of proportion won't apply due to foreshortening, and the parts of the body closest to us will appear larger than the parts further away.

In this illustration, the feet are much larger than they would appear if the person was standing up. The leg is shortened as well because we are looking straight at it. This is where your measuring skills are very useful, so you can see how long the leg really is in comparison to the foot and the body.

Shading can help make foreshortening make sense as well. It adds to the depth and distance of the work.

# Gesture drawing

These are super-quick drawings with the aim being to catch the movement of the pose. They're great for training the eye to draw action and become familiar with the body in all its angles.

Start with a stick figure to capture the basic pose and movement. Then begin to flesh it out. Use quick sketchy lines to find where the line should lie. This can also create the illusion of movement. Don't spend longer than five minutes on any drawing.

Try drawing on location with your visual diary and capturing the people passing by. Sporting events can be great. Or if you're sitting at a café, drawing while enjoying coffee and cake is a fabulous way to spend the afternoon!

# Animals

Drawing animals uses exactly the same skills and principles as we've used for all the other subjects. Measurement skills are particularly important, as the viewer will know if the proportions are incorrect more than they would with a generic vase.

Becoming familiar with the anatomy of various animals can be helpful. But the best thing is observation. Try drawing your family pet, or visit your friends and draw their pet as a present for them.

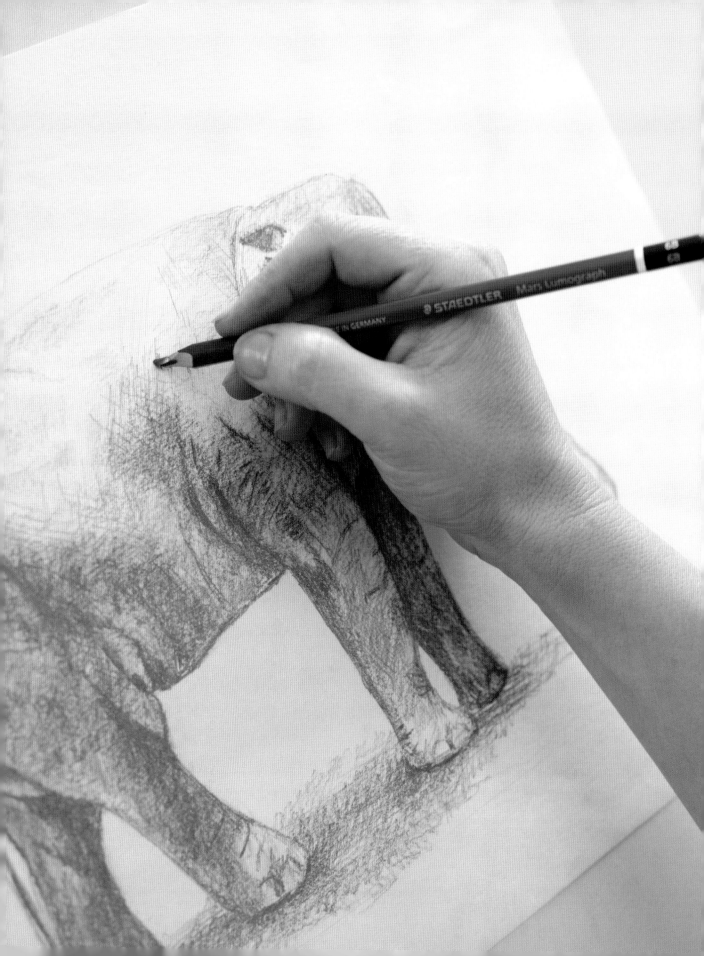

Going to the zoo is a great place to start drawing animals as well as a terrific day out. Take your visual diary to sketch in, and your camera so you can have a backup reference when you get home.

Try some of the animals that are fairly stationary first. Lions can be quite sleepy and will often stay still for lengths of time while you draw.

Following the same format as our other drawings, start by loosely sketching the shape, making sure the proportions look right. Add tone using a looser and more fluid style for the mane.

Elephants, with fabulous crevices and crinkles in their skin, are also great to draw.

Once again, the general shape is sketched. Notice the proportion of the ears to the head and the layers of skin bordering the gentle eyes. Add tone, making sure that the crevices retain their form.

When you're at home, using a reference from books or photos can be great practice, giving you time to focus on details and textures.

# Landscapes

There's a whole world out there waiting for you to draw it. You may see fantastic landscapes when you are travelling, but sometimes amazing landscapes can be just outside your front door if you look around. They can be the beach, a lovely park, or even the haphazard towers of the city.

Drawing landscapes is great for developing your compositional skills. One particular scene can often be broken down into a number of different possibilities and you have the exciting job of deciding which one you'd like.

Your framing device is great in this sort of situation and helps you to play around with a whole gamut of compositions. Drawing quick thumbnails is helpful in finalising your decision as to what works best.

# The natural landscape

This landscape is right near where I live. I chose a time of day that suited the mood I was after. Late in the afternoon near sunset provided a lovely soft light with interesting long shadows.

As with all my other drawings, I lightly sketched it first, making sure my marks were light enough to change if need be. The great thing about a landscape is that you can be a little looser with the proportions. Nobody will know if the tree you're drawing is bigger than it actually is. As long as it makes sense altogether, that's the main thing.

The branches in the foreground help break up the composition and, by having the larger object towards the front, give depth to everything else. The landscape becomes smaller, receding into the distance.

Next I started to add in more detail. When drawing trees, you don't have to draw in every leaf. In fact it will look forced if you do. Look at the general pattern that the trees make and imitate that. Each type of tree will have its own pattern in how the leaves group together. Some may need squiggles to create the effect; some may need flicks. Most trees have gaps in the foliage where the sky shows through. Just as if you were drawing an object, start to add in tone. Notice how the trees have dark and light patches. Sometimes people get so caught up in drawing the detail on trees they forget to shade these variations and the trees lose form.

As they recede, landscapes often become lighter and the atmosphere is less distinct. Use your tone to show this and make it blurrier as it goes back with less defined lines. This will add to the depth of your drawing.

Enhance the depth and dark tones using a full range of pencils. Pick out the highlights with your kneadable eraser and use the paper stump on the blurrier bits in the background.

With a sharp pencil, redefine the foreground objects, making sure they're sharply in focus.

# The urban landscape

Urban landscapes have a real diversity of moods. They can be fast and manic, or detailed in architecture and form. They're great for developing your perspective skills and, as most buildings have square shapes and blocks, it's easy to apply the rules you have learnt.

With this landscape, I blocked in the basic shapes of the landscape, drawing it first as squares and shapes so I could check that the perspective was correct.

Once I was satisfied, I started to add the detail, with windows and trimming on the buildings and cars.

Finally I added tone and then built up the detail again where it had become lost as I shaded in the highlights and lowlights. Using a sharp pencil, I pulled out the detail on the foreground buildings and softened the detail on the buildings in the distance with a paper stump.

To make an urban landscape fascinating for the viewer, pay attention to detail. The more of the tiny nooks and crevices you put in the better.

# Sketching Where You Go

Start taking your sketchbook out with you so you can jot down images whenever it takes your fancy – people, cars, animals … anything! Your eyes are your best drawing tool, so put them to good use.

Practise drawing a whole variety of things, such as different leaves and flowers. Look at their distinctive shapes and details. It's the minutiae in all these objects that make them interesting.

The more you sketch the better you'll become and you'll end up with a collection of fabulous books that document your drawing career.

# Time to Branch Out

Experiment with papers, pencils, charcoals and anything available at your local art shop that looks fun.

Try papers with a variety of different surfaces and colours. You'll end up with some lovely surprises once you start experimenting. Everything has been black and white till now, so like Dorothy from *The Wizard of Oz* you can now move into colour!

Charcoal and pastel are great for large drawings and can give a beautiful, free result. And watercolour pencils, inks and markers all have their own unique look.

Check out various artistic styles as well. Visit the gallery and see how many different types of drawings you can find. Till now we've only looked at realism, but experiment with abstract and expressionist styles if you like them.

Most importantly, have a wonderful time in this amazing world of discovery and embark on a lifetime adventure in art!

# About the Author

Jacqui Grantford has worked extensively as an artist, author and illustrator. She began her career working as a music teacher, but when her first-born cried every time she played the violin, she made the decision to move into the visual arts. She spent two years sleeping in the lounge room so she could use the bedroom as a working space, but now has a gorgeous, very messy studio that she treasures dearly.

Jacqui has had many books published and her work has been included in calendars, brochures and cards. She has won several prestigious artistic and publishing awards for her work.

One of Jacqui's greatest joys is to spend her time sketching and painting and she shares this passion through her work teaching both children and adults. She has taught all ages in most mediums and loves the challenge of inspiring her students. Jacqui feels that seeing someone's face light up as they produce a piece of work they're proud of is a deeply rewarding experience.

Jacqui currently announces on the radio show 'Classically Melbourne' on 3MBS FM, and continues her love of music.